C000264441

ENGLISH COUNTRY TOWNS

JOHN CURTIS

Text by Richard Ashby

SALMON

INTRODUCTION

A town is a place where traders meet to sell and to buy. Many grew up around an important castle or a monastery, others were situated where a river could be forded, where important roads met or where boats could be unloaded. Most received royal charters allowing them to hold markets and many also became important commercial, administrative and social centres for the surrounding countryside.

Country towns offer a fascinating panorama of English vernacular architecture. While stone was usually used for the most important buildings, even that was sometimes too expensive and flint or even brick was used instead. Timber framing was used for more domestic buildings. In the east of England it was usually hidden under plaster to stop the draughts, which are a hazard of such buildings, but in other areas the timber was also used decoratively and the elaborate timbers are exposed for the delight of all. English towns continue to evolve due to industrialisation, 'redevelopment', traffic and road schemes and particularly the inroads of 'out of town' shopping. However, there are still many towns, which have retained their essential character, where local shops, restaurants and pubs flourish and which celebrate with literary, music and other festivals. Most have thriving local societies dedicated to the conserving of all that is good about living in such proud and well-loved communities.

Ross-on-Wye, *Herefordshire*

WISBECH, *Cambridgeshire*
Wisbech was once on the coast but the sea has receded and is now some 10 miles away. Many English towns turn their backs to their rivers but at Wisbech handsome Georgian houses are ranged along the two 'Brinks', with the tidal Nene flowing between them.

BURY ST EDMUNDS, *Suffolk*
Bury was planned and laid out by the Normans in front of the great Abbey. In spite of a fire in the early 17th century the town was largely rebuilt in wood, but by the 18th century brick had become popular, often covered in Suffolk pink stucco.

SANDWICH, *Kent*

Sandwich was once a port but by the 16th century the River Stour was silting up leaving the little Cinque Port two miles from the sea and the trade went elsewhere. It was attacked by the French on a number of occasions, notably in 1447 when the Mayor was killed; his successors still wear black to this day.

MARLBOROUGH, *Wiltshire*

An important stop on the coach road from London to Bristol, Marlborough is a handsome town, with a church at each end of its wide High Street. A number of fires in the 17th century led to much rebuilding and the prohibition of thatch. As a result most of its buildings are Georgian or later.

OUNDLE, *Northamptonshire*

This old town reached its peak in the 17th and 18th centuries when many of the existing buildings were erected. It has fine coaching inns and Georgian shop windows. The buildings of the great public school, some of which date from the 16th century, are integral to the town,

HENLEY-ON-THAMES, *Oxfordshire*

Three counties, Oxfordshire, Berkshire and Buckinghamshire meet at this old market town, an important stopping place on the way from London to Oxford. The Thames could be bridged here and the river has always been important to Henley. It is the home of rowing and hosts the world famous regatta.

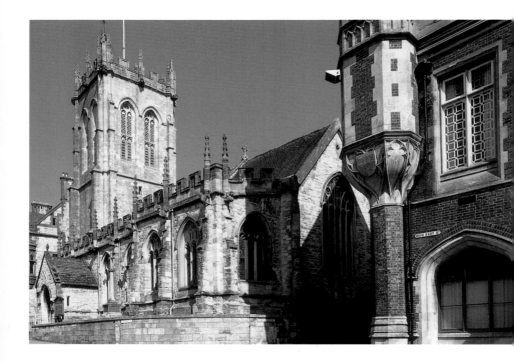

DORCHESTER, *Dorset*

Dorchester is the county town of Dorset and forever linked to the author Thomas Hardy who called it 'Casterbridge' in his novels. Hardy went to school in the town and later practised as an architect here. Many of the buildings described in his novels can still be recognised.

STAMFORD, *Lincolnshire*

Stamford is situated on the Great North Road, from London to York where there was a ford across the River Welland. The cloth made here was of the finest quality and was used by Cardinal Wolsey for the tents of the 'Field of the Cloth of Gold', when Henry VIII met the King of France.

APPLEBY-IN-WESTMORLAND, *Cumbria*

The famous Horse Fair, held outside this little north Pennine town every June, has drawn gypsies and travellers from all over the UK and from further afield, for over 200 years. Alongside the trade in horses and the colourful caravans there is plenty of entertainment with gypsy crafts, races, fortune telling and palm reading.

ALNWICK, *Northumberland*

Nestling up against its castle, Alnwick is an attractive stone-built Georgian town. As is common in northern England, street names often end in the Icelandic word 'gate', meaning 'passage'. Bondgate is where those who were 'bonded' or bound to the Duke of Northumberland in service lived.

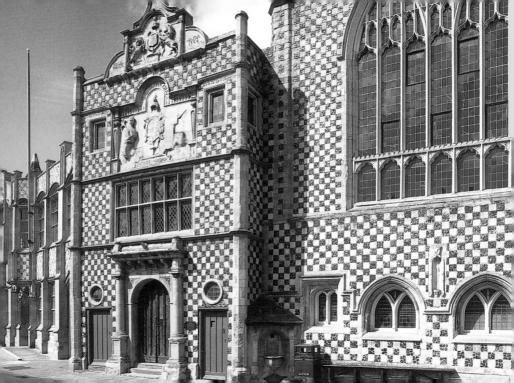

KING'S LYNN, *Norfolk*

Established at the mouth of the River Great Ouse near where it flows into the Wash, King's Lynn grew rich on its comparatively easy access to a large area of eastern England, exchanging wool, cloth and grain for timber and fish from north Germany and the Baltic and importing wine from France. Indeed, so important was it that in the late Middle Ages, King's Lynn was one of the few English ports to be a member of the Hanseatic League, which bound together the merchants of northern Europe and the Baltic for security and profit. This international trade has left a legacy of impressive warehouses, churches and civic buildings, all with a vaguely northern European air reflecting the trade across the North Sea.

WARWICK, *Warwickshire*

In spite of its enormous size the castle does not dominate Warwick, indeed it cannot be seen from much of the town. There was a great fire here in 1694 but some important 14th century buildings survive. This Chantry Chapel is over the town's west gate and next to it is Lord Leycester Hospital for aged and disabled soldiers, once the home of priests of the town's United Guilds. Founded in 1571 by Robert Dudley, Earl of Leycester it is still home to a number of ex-servicemen who help in the running of the hospital.

BAKEWELL, *Derbyshire*

Immortalised by the pudding (not a tart!) called by its name, it is now largely forgotten that Bakewell once had aspirations to be a spa. It is called 'Bedequella' in the Doomsday Book, meaning the 'bath-well' from the local warm springs which bubble up from the limestone below. The Romans, no doubt, enjoyed them but the later efforts to establish a spa left little to show compared to the glories of Bath or Harrogate. Rather, the town is a fine example of a prosperous, stone-built Derbyshire market town. It dates from Saxon times and, like Amersham, was granted a charter in 1200 and still has a weekly market. The town remained essentially medieval until the end of the 18th century but was then largely rebuilt. It lies in a narrow valley with water meadows nearby and is surrounded by the Derbyshire hills, which tower above it.

AMERSHAM, *Buckinghamshire*

Until the recent growth of suburbia, the Chiltern Hills were sparsely populated, largely through a lack of water. Amersham grew up alongside the stream, the Misbourne, which remains an important feature of its townscape.

RICHMOND, *Yorkshire*

In Norman-French Riche-Mont means 'Noble Hill'. The houses of Richmond cluster below the castle and cling to the steep sides of the mount on which it is built. Many of Richmond's streets are steep and paved with cobbles. Celia Fiennes, the pioneer 18th century female traveller, described them as 'like rocks themselves'

LEDBURY, *Herefordshire*

In many parts of England timber-framed buildings were plastered and the wood hidden. In Herefordshire, however, the timber frame was intended to be seen. Church Lane shows what the streets of many medieval towns must have been like before they were swept away by fires and the passion for improvement.

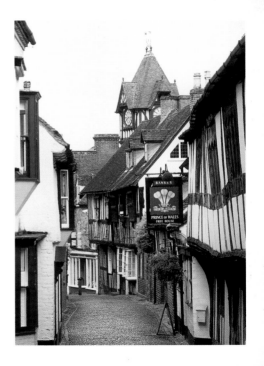

DISS, *Norfolk*

The river Waveney separates the counties of Norfolk and Suffolk. Diss is situated on the northern bank of one of the deepest natural inland lakes in the country. The market, which dates back over 500 years, is still flourishing and has recently been joined by regular antiques fairs, flea markets and a farmers' market attracting many visitors.

RYE, *East Sussex*

Although now some two miles from the sea, Rye retains its pride as one of the Cinque Ports. Visitors are attracted by its narrow cobbled streets and literary associations. Henry James, and after him E F Benson, lived in Lamb House and the notorious novelist, Radclyffe Hall, was once a resident.

BERWICK-ON-TWEED, *Northumberland*

Berwick deserves to be better known for it is a town of considerable interest. It is laid out on a grid plan which dates back to 1296 and has the first purpose-built army barracks in England, designed by Sir John Vanbrugh. The 18th century prosperity is reflected in the distinguished houses near the harbour, built for the prosperous merchant sea traders.

BEVERLEY, *North Yorkshire*

Beverley is famous for its Minster church, undoubtedly one of the finest parish churches in the country, which reflects the prosperity brought by wool. With the decline of the woollen industry and the rise of nearby Hull, the town settled into being a prosperous market and trading centre for the surrounding rich farmland.

BURFORD, *Oxfordshire*

Burford has long been known as the 'Gateway to the Cotswolds'. Its long main street rises up the hill from the river bridge and church. Largely built of the local honey-coloured stone, there are also many surviving half-timbered buildings. The town was bypassed by the railway and survived into the 20th century relatively unspoiled by Victorian commerce and industry.

SAFFRON WALDEN, *Essex*

The county of Essex has avoided many of the worst influences of London, and has some surprisingly attractive countryside and many lovely towns. Saffron Walden is one of these. Its many narrow alleyways, with their half-timbered buildings and their antique and bookshops, lead off the market place and are named after the various trades in which each specialised. The town was known as 'Chipping' Walden in the 14th century, reflecting its importance as a market centre (Cheyping means 'to buy' in Anglo-Saxon). By Tudor times the cultivation of the saffron crocus for its yellow dye, used in cloth making, had come to dominate the town and may well have lead to the change of name.

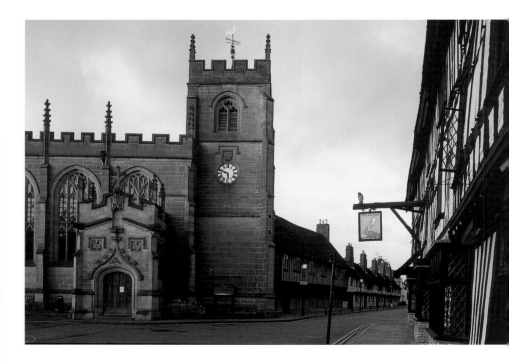

STRATFORD-ON-AVON, *Warwickshire*

Famed as the birthplace of William Shakespeare, there are reminders of Stratford's most famous son everywhere. A pleasant Midland's market town, its charter dates back to the 12th century and it was a prosperous place even before the plays of the Bard made it a place of pilgrimage. There are numerous Shakespeare sites, his birthplace, as well as that of his wife, the school he is believed to have attended and his tomb in the Parish Church.

LEWES, *East Sussex*

Lewes is a hill-top town, on a spur of the South Downs, with, at its centre, the remains of a Norman Castle which dominates the surrounding area. Chalk cannot be used for building but the flints which are found in it are a useful substitute and have been used for the castle and much of the town.

LUDLOW, *Shropshire*

Ludlow is another planned town. It is dominated by the Norman castle, which towers above a bend of the River Teme, and once commanded a strong position in the Welsh Marshes. The town provided services to the castle but soon became important in its own right. The wool trade brought great prosperity, which is reflected in the soaring tower of the church, in the main streets, where the timber-framed houses are a riot of pattern, and in some of the more modest domestic buildings. Only 30 miles from Birmingham, Ludlow retains its harmony and integrity and is no mere commuter town. Along with the many local shops, which survive and prosper, an increasing number of top quality restaurants attract discerning diners. At the end of June there is a two-week Festival of Music and Drama, the centre point of which is the castle itself.

LYMINGTON, *Hampshire*

This little port was once busy exporting timber, bricks and salt from the local salt marshes. The harbour is still one of the busiest on the south coast but is now filled with leisure craft. The old Georgian town, with its quaint cobbled streets, was once a haven for smugglers. The television series 'Howards Way' was filmed here.

BARNARD CASTLE, *County Durham*
'Barney' grew up around the castle stronghold begun by Bernard de Balliol, from whom it took its name. The ground floor of the Market Cross was used for the sale of dairy produce while the first floor was used as a gaol and later as a courtroom.

OAKHAM, *Rutland*
Oakham is the county town of Rutland, England's smallest county. It is built of the rich honey-coloured local ironstone. Near this Market Cross the stocks survive, once an incentive to the traders' honesty. Unusually, they are sheltered by a little roof.

BRADFORD-ON-AVON, *Wiltshire*

Bradford is an ancient town. The Saxons established a monastery here and a settlement grew
up nearby, where the road slopes down from the Cotswolds and crosses the Avon by means of a
'broad ford'. The ford was replaced by a bridge in the 13th century. A little chapel on the bridge
became a gaol in the 17th century. There are many fine Georgian houses overlooking the town.

Published in Great Britain by J. Salmon Ltd., Sevenoaks, Kent TN13 1BB. Telephone 01732 452381. Email enquiries@jsalmon.co.uk.
Design by John Curtis. Text and photographs © John Curtis. All rights reserved. No part of this book may be produced, stored in a
retrieval system or transmitted in any form or by any means without prior written permission of the publishers.
ISBN 1-84640-034-1   Printed in Slovenia © 2006

Title page photograph: Totnes, *Devon*
Front cover photograph: Shaftesbury, *Dorset*.   Back cover photograph: Shrewsbury, *Shropshire*